A SPECK IN THE UNIVERSE

The Bible on Self-esteem and Peer Pressure

ISBN 978-1-949628-17-3
Printed in the United States of America.
10 9 8 7 6 5 4 3 2 1   22 21 20 19

Published by The Pastoral Center, http://pastoral.center.

Developed in partnership with MennoMedia and Brethren Press. Series editors: Fumiaki Tosu, Ann Naffziger, and Paul Canavese. *A Speck in the Universe:* Writer, Steve Ropp. Project editor, Lani Wright. Staff editors, Susan E. Janzen, Julie Garber, and James Deaton. Updated design, Paul Stocksdale.

All rights reserved. Purchase of this book includes a license to reproduce this resource for use in a single parish, school, or other similar organization. You are allowed to share and make unlimited copies only for use within the organization that licensed it. If you serve more than one organization, each should purchase its own license. You may not post this document to any web site without explicit permission to do so. Outside of these conditions, no part of this book may be reproduced in any form or by any means, electronic or mechanical, including photocopying, recording, taping, or via any retrieval system, without the written permission of The Pastoral Center, 1212 Versailles Ave., Alameda, CA 94501. Thank you for cooperating with our honor system regarding our licenses.

For questions or to order additional copies or licenses, please call 1-844-727-8672 or visit http://pastoral.center.

Portions of this work © 2019 by The Pastoral Center / PastoralCenter.com. Adapted and published with permission from Generation Why Bible Studies. © 1996, 2014 Brethren Press, Elgin, IL 60120 and MennoMedia, Harrisonburg, VA 22803, U.S.A. All rights reserved.

Unless otherwise noted, the Scripture passages contained herein are from the *New Revised Standard Version of the Bible*, copyright © 1989 by the National Council of the Churches of Christ in the United States of America. Used by permission. All rights reserved.

Bible-based Explorations of Issues Facing Youth

» OVERVIEW

When conversing online, the acronym IRL stands for "in real life." The virtual world of social media, text chats, blogs, and more have the power to remove us from the real world. What we experience online can skew our perspective on what it means to be human. It can numb us, incite us, distract us, depress us, confuse us, and make us rude or impatient. Strangely, this supposedly "social" and "connected" technology can profoundly disconnect us from others.

Religious faith can also place us in a bubble, especially when it distances us from others. When we keep the prophetic message at a safe distance, obscured in theological language and abstractions, we are missing the whole point. And when we see our parish as an insider club that serves itself, we can forget the radically inclusive message entrusted to us: God's love is for *everyone*, and God expects us to transform the *whole world* through that love.

Through the incarnation, God showed up in the real world to show us that our faith is not just about talking the talk, but also walking the walk. It can be risky. It can be confusing. It can hurt. But living out our faith can also bring us great purpose, peace, and joy.

This series connects the Bible with the tough questions that youth (and adults) encounter in their neighborhood, in school, among friends, and even online. This process will help you as a leader break open these issues in a fun and meaningful way, sparking conversation and the kind of life change Jesus invites us to embrace.

» THE ROLE OF PARENTS

As children enter middle school and high school, they become more independent, self-reliant, and, well, self-centered. This can bring parents to make assumptions that this is the time to step back, giving their child more space to form their identity. While there is truth to that at some level (adolescents definitely shouldn't be smothered), this is a stage of life when parents should in fact *lean in*. The apparent confidence and bluster youth show on the outside can mask the insecurity and confusion on the inside. Youth need their parents to be involved more than ever.

» WHOLE FAMILY FORMATION

Parents are the primary teachers of their own children, and parishes are waking up to the fact that faith formation programs need to bring parents into the process if they hope to see faith passed on to the next generation. Recent studies give us more and more evidence that the role of parents is the most important factor in determining whether a child will embrace faith as they move toward adulthood. Research from the Center for the Applied Research on the Apostolate shows that parents who talk about their faith and show through their actions that their faith is important to them are more likely to have children who remain Catholic.

More about Whole Family Formation >>>>

To learn more about how your parish can take a comprehensive whole family approach to faith formation, visit **GrowingUpCatholic.com**.

While whole family events with elementary-aged children are on the rise, the role of parents can be an afterthought in youth ministry. We have designed the sessions in this series to work with or without parents present, and we encourage you to offer them as parent-child events.

If you choose to involve parents, it is important to consider before each session how to best do so. Many of the activities in this series are high-energy, creative, or silly. Some parents may need some encouragement to get out of their heads and have fun with the group. A few activities involving physical contact would be inappropriate for parents and youth to participate together, and we have noted them as such.

There are a number of ways to approach discussions with parent participation. Unless you have a small group, you will likely want to break into smaller groups for conversation. Some youth may be self-conscious and unable to be completely honest and open in a group situation with a parent present. For this reason, you may choose in some cases to assign parents to different groups from their own children, or to have separate parent and child groups altogether. Be sure to cover expectations around confidentiality. It is inappropriate for a parent (or youth) to share with another parent what their child said in a small group.

Note that even if parents and their children do not share all conversations together in the session, they will still have a valuable shared experience and can have extended conversations about it later.

>> THANK YOU

The role you play in gathering, animating, praying with, and forming youth is a valuable one. Thank you for all you do to serve the church and its families!

Bible-based Explorations of Issues Facing Youth

A SPECK IN THE UNIVERSE

The Bible on Self-esteem and Peer Pressure

>> INTRODUCTION

We are next to nothing in the grand scheme of the universe—just specks. In the breadth of space and time, we humans barely merit a glance. Yet in all this vastness, our God chose *humans* for a special relationship, and loved us through life, death, and back into life. Why would the great Creator of the universe do such a thing? Maybe there's something to us after all.

Self-esteem generally means that a person's worth comes from within. For believers, there is another, more important element: Our significance is rooted in being creatures of our awesome Creator and we, too, are proclaimed "good." It is not only who we are inside that gives us significance, it is "whose" we are—God's children.

Some speak of self-esteem in terms of high and low. How about seeing it as healthy and unhealthy? A person's self-esteem can be built up by telling them they are great, or they did a wonderful job; just as easily their esteem can take a hit by informing them they are stupid or clumsy. Healthy self-esteem can be nurtured by giving *both* praise and critique—the added ingredient is information. Let others know *why* you feel they did a good job, *why* they are wonderful people. Critique is easier to take and more productive when accompanied with care and concern for the individual. Take time to evaluate *why* something didn't turn out so well. Information helps a person decide how they will behave and respond in the future, giving them self-control and thus boosting self-esteem.

Self-esteem also hinges on who a young person sees in the mirror. Society today sends a lot of different messages, many defining what we need to be "somebody" and who we should be. God has a different message. This unit aims to help you get that message across. Building healthy self-esteem is about teaching people the skills to deal with life, reassuring them that they have innate worth endowed by their Creator, that they are loved, that they have a place in the new community of grace. Then, when rough times come, they don't destroy the individual.

But of course, the church isn't the only entity preaching a place to belong. Teens experience intense pressure from peers; often at this age, their friends have as much or more influence on them than their families. But pressure's also been around a long time. With this unit, you and your participants will study stories of biblical characters who faced some incredible pressure. Each time God was faithful, and in turn called believers to be faithful, even in the midst of self-

EXTENDER SESSION

Extender sessions suggest special activities related to the issue of the unit. They help accommodate the diversity of parish schedules. Since each unit is undated, youth may study units in their entirety and still participate in special events of the parish that get scheduled simultaneously with youth group time. Extender sessions can be used anytime, but the one for this unit best follows **Session 1**. Calculate now whether or not you will be using the extender session.

doubt and the pressures of a changing world. In our faithfulness as creatures of the Creator, we find our self-worth and gain strength not only against the onslaught of society's pressures, but can even turn our confidence to helping others along those rocky paths—that's positive peer pressure!

THE TEACHING PLAN: The parts of the session guide

» **Faith story.** The session is rooted in this Bible passage.

» **Faith focus.** This is the story of the passage in a nutshell.

» **Session goal.** The entire session is built around this goal. What changes—in knowledge, attitude, and/or action—do you desire in your group?

» **Materials needed and advance preparation.** This is what you will need if the session is to go smoothly. You'll feel more at ease if you've taken care of these details before you meet your group.

» FROM LIFE TO BIBLE TO LIFE

The teaching plan we use is called *life-centered*. However, when we write each session, we always begin with Scripture. We ask, what does this particular passage say, especially to youth? Each session moves from life to Bible to life. So the Bible is really at the center of this way of teaching.

In every session we try to hit upon a tough question that participants might ask. Find out what questions on this issue are important for your group. Feel free to bring your own input and invite your group members to add their own experiences.

» TEACHING THE SESSION

The five step-by-step movements will carry you from *life to the Bible and back to life*. Each session takes about 45 to 50 minutes. If there is a handout sheet for the session, take note of any complementary activities and stories.

1. **Focus.** This activity is intended to create a friendly climate within the group and to draw attention to the issue.

2. **Connect.** Talking, drawing, role playing, and other activities invite participants to express their own life experience about the issue. Also use memory, reason, or imagination to get the group thinking about *why* they view the issue the way they do.

3. **Explore the Bible.** With a minimum of lecturing, dig into the faith story and search for answers to questions raised in the first activities. The Insights from Scripture section will help clarify the faith story. Help participants discover how the faith community understands the Bible passage.

4. **Apply** the faith story. This is the "aha!" moment when participants realize the faith story has wisdom for their lives.

5. **Respond.** What will the group do about the issue in light of what they have learned from their own experiences set alongside the faith story? At this point, the faith story becomes lived rather than a mere intellectual exercise.

» LOOK AHEAD

Here are reminders for what you need to do for the next session or two.

›› INSIGHTS FROM SCRIPTURE

Here is a resource for Explore the Bible. Don't try to use all the material given. Take what you need to lead the session and answer questions your group may have. Let the Insights section inspire you to think and study more about the passage for the session.

›› HANDOUT SHEETS

Occasionally, there will be a handout sheet to complement your session. If you choose to use this, you will need to make enough copies for the group. These sheets may include questions, stories, agree/disagree exercises, charts, pictures, and other materials to stimulate your group to think and discuss.

Generally, no participant preparation is required unless the session plan calls for you to contact selected group members for specific tasks.

>>> SESSION 1

A CROWN OF HONOR >>>

>>> KEY VERSES

What are human beings that you are mindful of them, mortals that you care for them? Yet you made them a little lower than God, and crowned them with glory and honor. (Psalm 8:4-5)

>>> FAITH STORY

Psalm 8

>>> FAITH FOCUS

God created the heavens and the earth, and trusted human beings with the care of the world. Out of the expanse of the universe, God chose people—us—for relationship. Therefore, we must have great worth. Our significance is rooted in being creatures of our awesome Creator and we, too, are proclaimed "good." It is not only who we are that gives us significance, it is "whose" we are—God's children.

>>> SESSION GOAL

Since youth often struggle with identity and a sense of self-worth, help them see how, though we are mere specks in the universe, we are created "very good," worthy to be here, and are intimately connected to the Creator who made such an amazing universe.

>>> Materials needed and advance preparation

- Solar system chart (see Focus for how to prepare it)
- Two pounds (or about 200) M&M's or other edible tidbits, divided into two bowls of 100 each (*Option C*, Focus)
- Copies of handout sheet for Session 1
- Pencils/Pens
- Bibles
- Newsprint/markers or chalk/chalkboard
- Writing paper, enough for one sheet per person

 # TEACHING PLAN

1. FOCUS 10-12 minutes

Prepare a solar system chart for Focus *Option B* or *D*: Use newsprint or tape individual sheets together, so you have one continuous piece 7'7" long (2 m, 28 cm). **Note:** You could put a tape measure on the floor with the planets labeled. One inch (2.5 centimeters) from the left end make a dot about the size of a penny. Label it with a big #1. Then place dots at the following distances from the outside of this first dot and number them (use large, legible numbers):

Feet/inches		Centimeters/meters
#2 - 1"	Mercury	2.5 cm
#3 - 2"	Venus	5 cm
#4 - 3"	Earth	7.5 cm
#5 - 4.75"	Mars	12.2 cm
#6 - 1'4"	Jupiter	41 cm
#7 - 2'4"	Saturn	71.5 cm
#8 - 4'10"	Uranus	1.5 m
#9 - 7'7"	Neptune	2 m, 38 cm

Hang this on a straight wall, or lay out flat on the floor where everyone can see it. Then choose **two or more** of the following options to demonstrate the magnitude of time and space. The eventual point: In all this vast universe, people were created for a special relationship with the Creator.

>>> **Option A:** Say, *I want you to stare at your thumbnail for a full 10 seconds. Ready, go.* Inform them they just watched their fingernails grow 130 angstroms. On the chalkboard write "1 angstrom = one ten-millionth of a centimeter." Their fingernails grow at 13 angstroms per second!

>>> **Option B:** Distribute copies of the handout sheet, and have participants do "The Obvious Quiz." When they are finished go over the answers. (There is no key because the answers are obvious.)

>>> **Option C:** Share the following information with the group:

If this bowl of M&M's equaled the mass of the sun, how many M&M's from the other bowl would equal the total mass of all the planets and the moons that orbit them? Have participants make guesses. **Answer:** One M&M would equal the mass of the planets, moons, etc. In other words, the sun is about 100 times the mass of the rest of our solar system. Share the M&M's.

>>> **Option D:** Point out:

- *There is a sun which exists in our galaxy that if you put its center at the center of our sun, its surface would be located at Jupiter (about the location of dot #6 on the 8 foot/2.4 meter scale).*
- *Using the 8 foot/2.4 meter scale of our solar system, the closest star, Alpha Centauri C, would be 13 miles (20.8 km) away. The next closest star, Bernard's Star, would be over 18 miles (28.8 km) away.*
- *Scientists estimate there are about 300 billion stars in our galaxy. They estimate there are over one hundred billion other galaxies in our universe, some with less than a billion stars, some with more than a trillion.*
- *The Andromeda Nebula galaxy is visible with the naked eye from the northern hemisphere. It is 2 million light years away (that's over 6 million miles using the 8 foot scale, 9.6 million km using the 2.4 m scale).*
- *If a star is 4 light years away, like Alpha Centauri C, then the light we see from it is 4 years old.*

2. CONNECT 5 minutes

Discuss the following questions:

- *What are your thoughts right now in regard to the size of our universe?*
- *In the scheme of the universe, how big are you?*
- *On an 8 foot/2.4 m scale, how many angstroms are you?*

LOOK AHEAD

For the next session, when you study Zacchaeus (a man short on self-esteem), you'll need a ladder for one of the options in Explore. Also round up some songbooks. Instruments are optional.

- Which best describes how you feel related to the size of the universe:
  1. Smaller than a hair on a gnat's head
  2. Less than sweat on an ameba
  3. Lower than a dust atom on the belly of a snake in a wheel rut
  4. Insignificant as a moisture molecule on the brow of a flea

Shift to the next activity by saying: *Our universe is a huge place. Its size is staggering. Yet out of the expanse of the universe, God chose people—us—for relationship. Therefore, we must have great worth. Where do we fit into the scheme of things?*

3. EXPLORE THE BIBLE 10 minutes

Read Psalm 8:3-8. Then discuss:

- Where has God placed us in the order of creation?
- What responsibilities has God given people?
- Why do you think God has trusted us with so much?

4. APPLY 10 minutes

Using the chalkboard, have participants list adjectives that describe God (loving, powerful, gracious, generous, forgiving, intimate, etc.). Now go through this list and have group members identify the things created in humans that reflect these attributes of God. Then discuss:

- You know the creation stories in Genesis tell us people are created in God's image. How does being created in God's image impact your feelings about yourself?
- How do you feel now compared to how you felt earlier? Bigger than a tree? More powerful than a locomotive? Able to leap tall buildings in a single bound?
- How does being created in God's image affect your life?
- Psalm 8 says we're crowned with glory and honor, only "a little lower than God." How important are you in God's creation, in the universe?

Draw the following diagram on the board:

No one is insignificant. [God] loves all of us with a special love; for him all of us are important: *you* are important! God counts on you for what you are, not for what you possess. In his eyes the clothes you wear or the kind of cell phone you use are of absoutely no concern. He doesn't care whether you are stylish or not; he cares about you! In his eyes, you are precious, and your value is inestimable."

Pope Francis

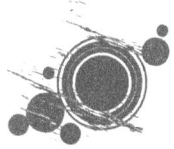

Explain the diagram something like this:

The outside circle of this diagram represents the behavior of a person, what we see him/her do, how they dress, how they talk, what they say, etc. Underneath the behavior are motivations; they prompt behavior. If a person feels worthwhile, you can see it in their behavior, right? Or maybe a person doesn't feel very good about themselves, so they put up a front. Their *unhealthy self-esteem motivates them to behave a certain way. Underneath motivations are values and beliefs. They lie closer to the core of what shapes us as human beings. If you believe it is wrong to kill someone, you will be motivated to behave a certain way. At the core of a person is spiritual identity. This is where the image of God dwells. Understanding that God created you not only helps you understand who you are, but **WHOSE** you are. You **ARE** a child of God. God created us out of love, and desires a relationship with us.*

5. RESPOND 10 minutes

There are times when we can really feel insignificant in the scheme of the universe. Yet we are created in the image of God. We carry a part of God in us. Now ask, *So what difference does it make if you're God's child?* Distribute paper and have participants choose one of the following:

- **a.** Describe, draw, sketch, etc. how they see themselves created in the image of God.
- **b.** Describe how being created in God's image impacts the way they see themselves.

As a group, list how this "image" affects each level of the diagram (values/beliefs, motivations, behavior). Finally, have everyone choose one thing from their list to pray for. Close in prayer, thanking God for creating us so "very good," asking for help in continuing to discover God's image in ourselves and others.

INSIGHTS FROM SCRIPTURE

How big is God? Science has helped us begin to grasp the enormity of space. Yet God is beyond space, beyond time. Then this great, beyond-thought God created the heavens and this earth, complete with day and night, water, land, and sky. After plants and animals, God created the crowning masterwork—people. All this creation God declared "very good." We are all created "good enough," with a right to be here in this world. This message, however, gets obscured with more negative ones.

The Genesis creation stories tell us that within each and every person born is God's image. Yet God is so huge, so expansive, no two people are alike. Each person carries "that of God" within. Being created in the image of God also means we are not our own. God is the one to whom we belong.

Set against the enormity of space, time, and all the wonders of earth, we can feel very small. The psalmist in Psalm 8:3-4 wonders, what could God have needed with yet one more creature? Echoing Genesis 1:28, the psalmist partly answers the question: God, for whatever mystery, needed humans to care for creation. The other part of the answer lies in God's nature. Our God is an intimate God, wishing to bestow love upon us, desiring a relationship with us. We are God's children, created to follow God.

When we look at the big picture, trying to comprehend our place in the universe, we must remember that God saw fit to create us. That we are images of such a stupendous God is where our self-worth comes from. Being God's creatures lays the foundation for all the self-esteem one could hope for.

›› REMEMBER WHO (AND WHOSE) YOU ARE

Youth and adults often forget their created image and get lost in a world that tries to tell them they are something else, or that they need to be a certain way to be something. Youth, especially, are torn by messages contradicting the goodness created in them. Beyond the shallow surface layer of behavior, past selfish motivations, through their values and beliefs and into their core being still lies the identity with which they were born: The image of God is central to who they are, making them a child of God. No longer is the question of "who am I?" the primary focus. The issue for all of us is "whose I am."

The OBVIOUS Quiz

Exploring tough questions facing youth today

1. Dot #1 is:
   a. really quite cute.
   b. On our scale model the location of the sun.

2. Dot #2 is:
   a. part human.
   b. On our scale model the location of Mercury from the sun.

3. Dot #3 is:
   a. all that's left of a smashed fly.
   b. On our scale model the location of Venus from the sun.

4. Dot #4 is:
   a. unique like a snowflake.
   b. On our scale model the location of Earth from the sun.

5. Dot #5 is:
   a. how big my pores are after a good workout.
   b. On our scale model the location of Mars from the sun.

6. In our solar system, the planets revolve around:
   a. the most conceited person in the room.
   b. the most beautiful person in the room.
   c. the Earth.
   d. the sun.

7. Dot #6 is:
   a. the size of the cavity in my back upper-left wisdom tooth.
   b. On our scale model the location of Jupiter from the sun.

8. Light travels at:
   a. the speed of sound.
   b. high speeds, but I can go faster.
   c. 186,282 miles (298,051 km) per second or over 5.88 trillion miles (9.41 trillion km) a year.
   d. so fast you can't see it.

9. Dot #7 is:
   a. The actual size of a black hole located in my closet.
   b. On our scale model the location of Saturn from the sun.

10. It takes light how long to get from the sun to Earth?
    a. Longer than it takes to get a pizza delivered.
    b. Faster than it takes to sneeze.
    c. Quicker than it takes me to irritate the person next to me.
    d. Eight minutes and 20 seconds.

11. How hot is the sun on its surface?
    a. Hotter than our teacher's car.
    b. Hot, but not as hot as the Phoenix Suns.
    c. Definitely hotter than the pizza we had delivered.
    d. 9300 degrees Fahrenheit, 5149 degrees Celsius.

12. The energy released from the sun is equivalent to:
    a. the horsepower of my car.
    b. the energy used to light up Las Vegas.
    c. what it takes to power my stereo.
    d. 100 billion one-megaton hydrogen bomb going off every second.

13. Dot #8 is:
    a. A good likeness of the mole on my left shoulder.
    b. On our scale model the location of Uranus from the sun.

14. Even though the sun uses up 600 million metric tons of hydrogen a second, it will continue to shine at its present brightness:
    a. not quite as long as my sister takes in the bathroom.
    b. longer than my dad can talk.
    c. not as long as this session will last.
    d. 6 billion years.

15. Our galaxy is:
    a. so big I prefer to drive from planet to planet.
    b. 100 light years in diameter.
    c. not as big as the Yukon and Alaska put together.
    d. not big enough for me and my brother/sister to coexist.

16. Our solar system is traveling through space around the center of the galaxy at:
    a. speeds you can't reach in a Chevy.
    b. a rate which causes me to take motion sickness pills.
    c. nothing near what I can do on my motorcycle.
    d. 170 miles (272 km) per second.

17. At the rate listed in question 16, it will take us how long to go around the center of the galaxy once?
    a. We should get around once before I get married.
    b. About as long as it takes me to dry my hair.
    c. Longer than it takes me to eat a pizza.
    d. Over 200 million years.

18. Dot #9 is:
    a. a figment of my imagination.
    b. On our scale model the location of Neptune from the sun.

19. Say you wanted to travel to the star which is closest to us, Alpha Centauri C. If you traveled at the speed of light, how long would it take for you to get there?
    a. Well, say you could travel at the speed of light, would you be able to see yourself in a mirror? If not, I don't think I want to travel to this star.
    b. Wouldn't you go backwards in time if you traveled at the speed of light? If you did, then you would never get there because you would have traveled back to before you left. What would happen if you met yourself going?
    c. Hey, I will go anywhere as long as it is expense paid and in the opposite direction of my parents.
    d. It would take you over 4.3 years.

A Speck in the Universe : Session 1

Permission is granted to photocopy this handout for use with this session.

>>> **SESSION 2**

LOVE FOR THE UNLOVED >>>

>>> KEY VERSE

Jesus said to him, "Today salvation has come to this house, because [Zacchaeus] too is a son of Abraham." (Luke 19:9)

>>> FAITH STORY

Luke 19:1-10

>>> FAITH FOCUS

Riches could not buy respect for Zacchaeus, a despised tax collector. Therefore, the locals were dismayed when Jesus asked to be a guest in Zacchaeus' home, for the tax collector was a swindler and a sinner. But in Jesus' presence, Zacchaeus turned from his cheating ways and experienced the long arms of God's love, which reaches to all who feel unloved.

>>> SESSION GOAL

With adolescence being a time of feeling unloved, help group members learn how to recognize and feel the love God has for them.

>>> Materials needed and advance preparation

- Set up the room with chairs in a circle, one per person.
- Chalkboard/chalk or newsprint/markers
- Half-sheets of paper, enough for one per person
- Pencils/pens
- Ladder (*Option A* in Explore the Bible)
- Bibles
- Hymnals/songbooks (guitar/instruments optional)

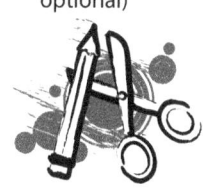

 **TEACHING PLAN**

1. FOCUS 7 minutes

Create one circle with enough chairs for each of the youth. If you are holding a whole family session, parents should sit this activity out. With the participants sitting in the circle of chairs, read the following "If you..." statements and have them move the direction and number of chairs indicated. (Participants may end up sitting on someone else's lap, maybe two, three, or four deep, so be prepared and have fun!).

- If you have ever had a crush on someone, move 2 chairs to the left.
- If you've ever practiced smooching by kissing your mirror, move one chair to the right.
- If you have ever dreamed about being with someone famous, move one chair to the left.
- If you have ever liked someone in a romantic sense, move three chairs to the right.

- If you have ever disliked someone so much you wanted to see them suffer, move two chairs to the right.
- If you can name a time you felt God's love for you, move one chair to the right.
- If you have ever loved anyone (parents included) move two chairs to the left.
- If someone has ever said they hated you, excluding your parents and siblings, move one chair to the left.
- If you have ever said "I hate you" to someone's face, move three chairs to the right.
- If someone has ever said they love you, excluding your parents, move one chair to the right.
- If you've ever received a love letter, email, or text, move three chairs to the left.

Small Group Option (for groups smaller than four): Make a circle of chairs, enough for one per person, *plus* two empty chairs. Proceed with the activity as outlined above. The chances of ending on someone's lap are slimmer, but the anticipation is also keener!

"God is looking for you, even if you do not seek Him. God loves you, even if you forget Him. God sees beauty in you, even if you think you have squandered all your talents in vain."

Pope Francis

2. CONNECT 5 minutes

>> **Option A:** On a newsprint or chalkboard, list different ways that love can be communicated to someone (spoken, written, hugs, etc.). Then list people in the news or in history that you'd find it really *hard* to love (political figures, sports figures, serial killers, etc.).

>> **Option B:** Discuss the following questions. If your group is particularly reserved, you may give them time jot down answers to the questions before asking them to share:

- *What are some ways you have felt loved?*
- *Where does love come from?*
- *How do we receive it?*
- *Why are some people easier to love than others?*
- *What makes people unlovable?*
- *Have you ever felt "unlovable"? Why or why not?*
- *What one person has loved you the most? Why?*

Shift to the next activity by saying: *There are many ways we feel loved, by many different people. Sometimes we feel unlovable and don't understand why anyone would want to love us. But God always loves us.*

3. EXPLORE THE BIBLE 8-10 minutes

>> **Option A:** Ask for volunteers to act out the Luke 19:1-10 passage. You will need someone to play Jesus, Zacchaeus, and several people in the crowd. If possible, re-enact the story outdoors, with Zacchaeus in a real tree. If this is not possible, have Zacchaeus on a ladder, or on someone's shoulders. Read the story, pausing where action is called for. If there is a spoken line, have the appropriate character repeat it after you have read it. Encourage the players to use emotion, and have them say it again if you would like them to add more emotion to the part.

>> **Option B:** Have the group list what they know about Zacchaeus on newsprint or the chalkboard. You might even sing the song "Zacchaeus Was a Wee Little Man" to jog their memories. Include things like: wealthy, short, curious, loved (by Jesus), unloved, unpopular, tax collector, saved, eager to make things right, etc. Say something like: *I wonder what it must have felt like to be Zacchaeus*, or *I wonder why Zacchaeus did what he did*. Allow time for responses.

4. APPLY 8 minutes

Survey your group using the following question: *On a scale of one to ten (ten being high) how much love did Jesus have for Zacchaeus? What evidence can you give for your answer?* Ask: *Does God love murderers? addicts? abusers? the rich? the poor? Why or why not?* If participants acknowledge that God can love any of these, point out that God must certainly love everyone here in your group!

Distribute half-sheets of paper and pencils, one per person. (If you are outdoors use rocks or sticks to make scratches on a sidewalk or in dirt.) Have everyone draw a line with a "1" at one end and a "10" at the other. With 10 being the highest, ask them to mark with an "x" the amount of love they feel God has for them.

Ask: *How much does God love you?* Encourage participants to share Bible verses or stories, experiences, or other significant insights. Ask: *What is required from us to receive God's love?* On the paper where they drew their line, have them mark with a "G" the amount of love God intends for them to feel. Have volunteers share where they marked their line with regard to the love they feel God has for them, and also the amount of love God intends them to feel. Have them explain any difference in their marks.

Note: This line of questioning has potential to be intensely personal, or for being an opportunity to witness to God's love. Be sensitive about the level of sharing you ask for.

5. RESPOND 10-15 minutes

On newsprint or chalkboard list **adjectives** describing God's love for us (awesome, unending, incomprehensible, etc.).

>> **Option A:** Using a songbook, or from memory, list songs that are about God's love for us. Have volunteers pick a song and sing it together as a group (use the books and an instrument if songs are not very familiar). What can be added to your list above about God's love for us? Sing as many songs as time allows.

>> **Option B:** Have participants write love letters from God to anonymous recipients. Give volunteers the opportunity to read theirs to the group. When finished, put these in an envelope and keep them for future use, such as when a group member is feeling unloved or if someone knows of someone else who might need to hear how God loves them.

Before closing in prayer, paraphrase John 3:16 to the group, saying something like: *God loves each of us so very much that God sent his son Jesus to show us the way to life, even at the risk of dying a painful, lonely death. God didn't go to all the trouble of sending Jesus merely to point an accusing finger, telling the world how bad it was. Jesus came to help, to put the world right again. Receiving and responding to this love brings abundant life.*

Ask: *Do you feel God's love differently now than at the beginning of our time together? Why or why not?*

Close in prayer, thanking God for the incredible love given to us. Ask God to help everyone present to experience the awesome, unending, overpowering love meant for them through the crucifixion of Jesus. Send them out with this assurance from Romans 8:38-39: *For I am convinced that neither death, nor life, nor angels, nor rulers, nor things present, nor things to come, nor powers, nor height, nor depth, nor anything else in all creation, will be able to separate us from the love of God in Christ Jesus our Lord.*

LOOK AHEAD

Next session includes an anointing service, for which you'll need olive oil or baby oil (scented if you like). Consider playing a recording of the song "Sanctuary" or "Holy Ground" in the background.

Could we with ink the ocean fill

And were the skies of parchment made,

Were every stalk on earth a quill

And every [one] a scribe by trade,

To write the love of God above

Would drain the ocean dry,

Nor could the scroll contain the whole

Though stretched from sky to sky.

Frederick M. Lehman,
"The Love of God"
(hymn text)

INSIGHTS FROM SCRIPTURE

It could read like tabloid news: *Local doctor and renowned preacher seen chumming it up with inhabitants at known crack house.* Change the context just a little, and you've got the shocking tabloid news of first-century Jericho: *Jesus caught eating with tax collectors and sinners.* Zacchaeus was a Jew who collected taxes for the occupation forces, the Romans. As much as the Jews hated paying taxes to Romans, they absolutely despised the turn-coat Jews who collected those taxes, typically lining their own pockets as well. Zacchaeus was an outcast, unloved by his own people, shacked up in their minds with robbers, adulterers, and traitors.

›› ZACCHAEUS: SHORT ON SELF-ESTEEM

Yet Zacchaeus had such strong desire to see Jesus that he would go out in public among people who hated him. When Jesus came by, he saw Zacchaeus and called him by name (divine knowledge or good reconnaissance by the disciples?). Of all the "righteous" people Jesus could have spent time with, he instead chose Zacchaeus. The more pious onlookers grumbled that Jesus chose a sinner to spend time with. Hearing this, Zacchaeus repented *on the spot*, promising to pay back (times four!) what he had unlawfully taken, as well as sharing his wealth with the poor. Jesus' response was not so much to Zacchaeus as to the crowd: that even Zacchaeus was a son of Abraham and his repentance made him eligible for salvation. Both Zacchaeus and the crowd witnessed that day how long is the reach of God's love, and how the realization of that love can change a person's life.

›› NEVER OUT OF REACH

In Romans 4, Paul establishes that we are *all* descendants of Abraham when we share the same faith. In Romans 8:35-39 Paul tells us **there is no power in this universe** that can separate us from God's love. There is nothing that can separate us from God and the fact we are God's children. God's love will be there for us through the end of the ages!

How much does God love us? The answer is in John 3:16. God loves us so much that God gave his only Son to give life to the world. Jesus the Messiah who came to save us all, gave his life. Most parents would find it impossible to imagine loving someone else so much they would give the life of one of their children to save the life of another. Yet God has so much love for you and me that Jesus was not just killed, but allowed to be crucified (one of the most humiliating, lonely, and painful ways to die) so we can have eternal life. What more can be said? What more can be done? Christ died for all of us, the lovable and unlovable.

SESSION 3

ON BEING HOLY >>>

>> KEY VERSES

For God called us to holiness, not to impurity. (1 Thessalonians 4:7, NEB)

>> FAITH STORY

Judges 13–16; 1 Thessalonians 4:3-8

>> FAITH FOCUS

Samson was given great strength as long as he remained true to God's instructions, and God dwelled in him during his faithfulness. Samson's strength, as well as his healthy self-esteem, was dependent on his being indwelt with God's spirit. Like Samson, we are called to be holy. But there's no room for God to dwell if a person is filled up with other junk.

>> SESSION GOAL

Help youth boost their self-esteem by keeping clean the "temples" of their bodies, since they are a sacred dwelling place for God.

>> Materials needed and advance preparation

- Locate a fairly uncluttered closet or small room in your building, small enough so that not quite everyone could fit in (*Option C* in Focus).
- Newsprint/markers or chalkboard/chalk
- Pencils
- Bibles
- Copies of handout sheet for session 3 (*Option A* in Respond)
- Envelopes
- Olive oil or baby oil for anointing
- Consider playing the song "Sanctuary" or "Holy Ground" in the background for anointing in Respond

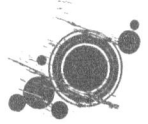

TEACHING PLAN

1. FOCUS 6-8 MINUTES

>> **Option A:** On newsprint or chalkboard have participants list special/important places in the world. Then ask:

- *Why are these places special or important?*
- *How are they cared for? What is done to keep them special? How much time and money do you think is spent keeping them in good shape?*
- *Are they guarded? Why?*

Make another list of places considered holy (set aside for God) or sacred. Ask:

- *Why are these places considered holy?*
- *How are they cared for?*

Go on to Connect *Option A*, below.

> "A tree gives glory to God by being a tree... For me to be a saint means to be myself. Therefore the problem of sanctity and salvation is in fact the problem of finding out who I am and of discovering my true self."

Thomas Merton
New Seeds of Contemplation

>> **Option B:** Enlist everyone's help in turning your meeting place into a "holy" place, a sacred dwelling place for God. What will you need to do? Then *do* it! Things to consider:

- What objects need to be put into the room?
- How should the furniture be arranged?
- What is distracting and needs to be removed from the room?
- What should one's attitude be when entering a holy place?
- What does one wear in a holy place?
- What sounds do you want to add or remove?

Go on to Connect *Option A*, below.

>> **Option C:** Find a fairly uncluttered closet or small room in your building, small enough so that not quite everyone could fit in. See if you can fit everyone from your group into this space. When you are scrunched in or tired of scrunching, ask the questions under Connect *Option B*.

2. CONNECT 3-5 minutes

>> **Option A:** (for *Option A* or *B* of Focus) Ask participants if they consider anyone they know to be holy, a person who lives a godly life. Say: *I wonder why they are holy?* and give them opportunity to respond. Now ask them if they consider themselves to be holy and say: *I wonder why that is?* and give them time to respond. Then ask:

- *What makes a person "holy"?*
- *Is it easy to be a holy person?*
- *Can anyone be holy?*
- *Can you be holy and still be doing everything you like or want to do?*
- *What does a person need to do to prepare themselves to be a dwelling place for God?*

>> **Option B:** (questions for the closet):

- *How easy or hard was it to get everyone into the space provided?*
- *Who or what had to be left out?*
- *What would it have taken to fit everyone into the space?*
- *Imagine that your **body** is that closet, and God is trying to get in. Could God fit into you and live there? Why or why not?* (Point out that that's what being holy is—making room in your life, even in your body, for God to dwell in you.)

Shift to the next activity by saying: *It isn't always easy to be holy. There are many stories in the Bible of people who were holy, but also failed God at times. Let's take a look at one of them.*

3. EXPLORE THE BIBLE 15-17 minutes

Distribute Bibles. If you have a large group, divide into four subgroups. Have each group read one of the chapters from Judges, below. For smaller groups, divide up the chapters one to a person, or as you feel is appropriate. Give each group a pencil and paper and ask them to note their reaction to the stories of Samson. What do they like about Samson? Dislike? What do they notice in the stories that is new to them? Ask them to be prepared to retell what they read and to share what they learned about Samson.

- Judges 13
- Judges 14
- Judges 15
- Judges 16

As a whole group, discuss:

- *What were the instructions given to Samson's mother?*
- *What was Samson like?*
- *What made him strong?*
- *What caused him to become weak?*
- *What influence did others have on him?*
- *What made Samson "set aside"?* (Answer: no alcohol, no touching dead bodies, not cutting hair.) *Are these "holy" acts?* (No, but being obedient to God is.) *What happened to Samson when he gave away his secret?*
- *Did God want Samson to be perfect? faithful?*

Expand your discussion of what it means to be holy by looking at the following scriptures and discussing the questions:

Leviticus 20:7-8
Do we make ourselves holy? Why or why not?
What do we need to do to be holy?

Leviticus 20:26
Why are we holy?
Are we set apart? In what way?

1 Thessalonians 4:3-8
Does "knowing God" make a difference in our lives?
How would you describe someone who is sanctified or holy (set aside for God)?
What do you think it means to be "impure"?
What does God call us to do?

1 Peter 1:13-16
What steps do we need to take?
Who are we to be?
As children of God, why are we to be holy?
What happens to us when we go against God's instructions?

4. APPLY 10 minutes

>> **Option A:** Briefly discuss a few of the following questions:

- *What is the most important thing or things one needs in order to be holy?*
- *What can you do to help others be more holy?*
- *What has God given you that helps you be holy?*
- *What happens to us when we are not holy? How do we see ourselves? How do we feel about ourselves? What happens to our self-esteem?*

Then distribute copies of the handout sheet and have participants fill them out, including signing their names. Distribute envelopes and ask everyone to self-address them and put their papers inside. Collect them, assuring participants that you will keep them confidential. **Follow-up:** There is space for you to write an encouraging note on the holiness you see in them, affirming them as children of God, made in God's holy image. Mail them [use traditional mail; people enjoy receiving letters!] sometime early in the week so participants will be reminded and encouraged. If you can't send them, hand them out the next time you meet the group.

》》 Option B: Offer the following guided meditation to help participants visualize themselves as a cleaned-up, holy dwelling place for God, where God's power and strength can make them strong.   Invite everyone to sit comfortably, close eyes, and suggest that they sit with their palms up in their lap, as a posture of being open to receiving the Spirit. Then say the following, pausing for some moments at the end of each sentence.

Imagine you have been shrunk to the size of a pea. You are small enough now to take a trip inside yourself. You can go inside your body, or inside your spirit, whichever you like. Think of it as a sort of little room. What's that room inside you like? Is there a lot of stuff in there? Or is there hardly anything? What do you recognize? What colors are the walls? Are there windows? Furniture? Loud or soft music? Is there anything you are surprised to find? Is there anything you are happy to find? Sad to find? Anything you'd like to get rid of? Anything you'd like to put in there to make it more of a special place for you, a place that's just yours? What would that room be like if it reflected exactly who you are?

LOOK AHEAD

Ask two participants to come prepared to read the following Bible passages for next session: Luke 7:36-50 and Matthew 9:9-13. Also plant a couple of participants to be "shunners" (*Option B* under Focus, Session 4).

*Is God there? Would you **like** God to be there? Is there room for God amidst the things that are already there? Do you think God would be comfortable there? Is it a place you would like to have God see, this room that is your spirit inside? If so, imagine that God has come to live in that room, and that the two of you sit down together and have a good talk. If you aren't sure God is there, or aren't sure God could even get in the door, is there anything you'd like to change in the room so that it would be a good space for God? What would it be? What do you need to clean out in order for you to be a dwelling place for God? Now get up and leave your room for a time, closing the door behind you, knowing you can always go back to make changes, to welcome God, to remember who you really are. Join us in this group again.*

5. RESPOND 5-8 minutes

Anointing. (Consider playing the song "Sanctuary" or "Holy Ground" in the background.) Invite participants to pair up and stand facing each other. Pass around the oil, instructing everyone to put a little on the index and middle fingers. Then have them take turns placing their fingers on the other's forehead, and praying for that person to be a dwelling place for God, to clean out the junk inside so God can live in them, asking for strength to be a holy dwelling place for God. After the first person is done, the other repeats the process and prayer.

Note: If participants do not feel comfortable praying for each other, you as leader can pray aloud as they place the oil on each other's foreheads, while others pray silently with you.

 INSIGHTS FROM SCRIPTURE

As children of God, as creatures created in God's image, we are invited to be holy, mirroring the holiness of our Creator. When we align with God, keeping God's commandments and teachings, God creates holy space in us.

Samson's parents were given specific instructions on raising their longed-for son. He was to be a *nazirite*, one separated or consecrated to do God's will. Usually nazirites would take a special, voluntary vow to "separate themselves to the Lord" (Num. 6:2). The restrictions they took upon themselves, which included not cutting the hair, would last only for a time, and at the end of the period they would cut off the hair that had grown and devote it to God. "All their days as nazirites they are holy to the Lord" (Num. 6:8).

In Samson's case, however, he was to be holy, set apart and consecrated, a nazirite, *all* his life. In return, God gave him great strength as long as Samson remained faithful and true to God's instructions. But when Samson was pressured to give away his secret, he was compromised and lost his sense of God within him. His strength and power were gone.

The people of Israel were "set apart" so as to highlight God as unique and powerful among the many gods of the surrounding cultures. When they fell short, God sent Samson and others to get them back on task. But Samson's story shows the result of disobedience on both a personal and corporate level.

The Hebrew people had a very strong sense of identity as God's chosen people. For people today it isn't so easy or clear. By society's standards "who we are" is tied more to what possessions we *have* than to "whose we are." Holiness comes from acknowledging God as one's parent, creator, maker. We establish our identity through living as beloved children of God.

›› LIVE HOLY LIVES

God desires for us to be sanctified (1 Thes. 4:3). For this to happen, we need to learn self-control, to take care of ourselves, to live honorable lives. God calls us to live holy lives, not to be impure (1 Thes. 4:7). This is the responsibility we accept when we invite God into our lives, when we become part of Christ's body. Rejecting the call to live a holy life is rejecting God. Yet God does not leave us to struggle alone. The Holy Spirit is given to strengthen and guide us.

Living holy lives does not mean we never stumble. We will still have desires that are not of God. But when we choose God, we choose a path away from ignorance and toward wisdom and holiness. We know of God and God's holiness, so we, too, are to be holy because God is holy.

If we know, listen, and follow God we will be holy. A lot of what goes into making healthy self-esteem is a sense of physical well-being or inner strength. Youth need to make this connection, to hear: *Take back your life, your health; take back what's good for you, because you are meant for God's spirit to be dwelling in you.* With support and love, youth can live holy lives and make choices that will help them feel good about who they are and whose they are!

The earth is yours, O Giver of life, in all its fullness and glory, the world and all those who dwell therein; for you have founded it upon the seas and established it upon the rivers.

Who shall ascend your hill, O Gracious One, and who shall stand in your holy place?

All who have clean hands and pure hearts, who do not lift up their souls to what is false, nor make vows deceitfully.

All these will be blessed by the Heart of Love, and renewed through forgiveness.

Such is the promise to those who seek Love's face.

Psalm 24:1-6, *Psalms for Praying*, paraphrase by Nan C. Merrill

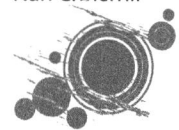

what's HOLY about me?

Exploring tough questions facing youth today

What I need to clean out to make room for God

_____
_____
_____
_____

What I can change beginning this week

_____
_____
_____
_____

The earth is yours, O Giver of life, in all its fullness and glory, the world and all those who dwell therein; for you have founded it upon the seas and established it upon the rivers.

Who shall ascend your hill, O Gracious One, and who shall stand in your holy place?

All who have clean hands and pure hearts, who do not lift up their souls to what is false, nor make vows deceitfully.

All these will be blessed by the Heart of Love, and renewed through forgiveness.

Such is the promise to those who seek Love's face.

Psalm 24:1-6, *Psalms for Praying*, paraphrase by Nan C. Merrill

A Speck in the Universe : Session 3

Permission is granted to photocopy this handout for use with this session.

>>> SESSION 4

THE 'IN' CROWD >>>

>> KEY VERSES

"You did not anoint my head with oil, but she has anointed my feet with ointment. Therefore, I tell you, her sins, which were many, have been forgiven; hence she has shown great love. But the one to whom little is forgiven, loves little." (Luke 7:46-47)

>> FAITH STORY

Luke 7:36-50; Matthew 9:9-13

>> FAITH FOCUS

Simon, considered righteous because he was a Pharisee, found from the example of a sinful woman what it meant to be forgiven and accepted into God's family. Jesus spent a lot of time eating, talking with, and healing people who were considered outsiders, and they responded with gratitude and love. Jesus treated them with love and respect, resulting in changed lives. Even when we feel outside of God's love and cast off by peers, we, too, can be restored to God. When we respond to God's love, God showers us with love.

>> SESSION GOAL

With youth struggling and searching for acceptance in social groups, give them a place to belong where they are accepted.

>> Materials needed and advance preparation

- Index cards
- Pencils
- Bibles
- Newsprint/markers or chalkboard/chalk
- One medium-size bag of M&M's or something similar
- Recruit "shunners" (*Option B* in Focus).

TEACHING PLAN

1. FOCUS 6-8 minutes

>> **Option A:** (for groups larger than 5):

Divide into groups of 5 or 6 (one group of 5 or 6 is fine). Take one youth (*not* someone who may already be a "fringe" member) from each group and have them leave the room. The job of the remaining participants is to keep the one from getting back into the group. They may want to huddle together and put their arms around each other. Go out of the room to the youth who left and inform them that their task is to get back into their group. As leader your job is to make sure everyone stays safe. Some youth will be quite aggressive in trying to get back into their group, others might not try at all. Ask:

- *How did it feel being left out?*
- *What did you do to try to get back into the group?*
- *What techniques were most effective at keeping the "outsider" out?*

- *If you got back in, did you feel like you were part of the group?*
- *How did it feel keeping someone out?*
- *How did you feel once they got in?*

 Option B: (for small or large groups):

Gather several participants prior to meeting and ask them to intentionally shun someone else from the group. This works best if the person being shunned is one of the more popular people. Have them do whatever they can to exclude the person from the usual circles. When your group convenes, talk with everyone except the one being left out, **ignoring them completely.** Offer food and drink, distribute supplies for the session, but leave out the person being shunned.

If you only have two or three youth in your group, choose carefully the person you will leave out. You may choose to talk only to one of the other youth about something you arranged with them prior to the meeting and leave the other one or two youth out of the conversation. Ask the following questions:

- *How did it feel being left out?*
- *Did you do anything to try and be part of the group? If so, did you really feel you were part of things?*
- *How did it feel to exclude someone? Was it easy or hard?*

2. CONNECT 5 minutes

Shift from the previous contrived experience to real life. Give everyone **three** M&M's. **No eating!** Ask if anyone has ever… (and give them an M&M for each "yes" answer)

- *experienced being on the outside of a group*
- *known their friends were going to a party but they weren't invited*
- *been laughed at by others*
- *been made fun of because of the way they were dressed*
- *been left out because of something they believed*
- *been picked last (or not at all) to play on a team*
- *been called bad names*
- *(add a couple of your own)*

Now *take away* an M&M for every "yes" answer:

- *made fun of someone else in the last week*
- *laughed at someone*
- *shared an inside joke with someone while they left another person out*
- *intentionally left someone out of an activity*
- *(add a couple of your own)*

Have each person count up how many M&M's they have. Have them remember their totals for later. Let people eat what they have.

Shift to the next activity by saying: *Being an "outsider" is rarely fun or easy, but an unseen advantage, even better than M&M's, is that you really know how to appreciate God's love.*

> "Compassion – it is a word meaning to suffer with. If we all carry a little of the burden, it will be lightened. If we share in the suffering of the world, then some will not have to endure so heavy an affliction."
>
> Dorothy Day
> *On Pilgrimage*

3. **EXPLORE THE BIBLE** 10-12 minutes

Distribute Bibles, and have the two people you solicited read the Luke 7:36-50 and Matthew 9:9-13 passages while others follow along. Ask: *What do you know about the people in these stories from what you've just heard?* List their responses on the chalkboard or newsprint under the following headings: **Simon, sinful woman, Matthew, Pharisees in general, Jesus, God**. As participants generate answers, supplement their responses with information from the Insights section. For more discussion, ask: *What (if anything) about each of these stories makes you feel depressed? feel hopeful?*

4. **APPLY** 10-12 minutes

>> **Option A:** Put the following statements up on the chalkboard or newsprint: **"Society says to be on the inside you must…"** and **"Jesus says to be on the inside you must…"** After hearing responses, discuss: *How can this group, or our church, be completely different from society, and be the place where people are accepted?*

>> **Option B:** If you feel your group needs to learn to be more sensitive to "outsiders," have them first identify people they consider outsiders, or social outcasts. They can be people they know or people who have been "sorted" by society. If you have a large group, divide into subgroups of 5-8 and have each group take someone or a group of people they have identified, instructing them to put together a short skit including characters who would treat them unkindly, laugh at them, etc. If your group has 5 or fewer people, simply choose one or two "outsiders" from the list. Then, have someone be the character of Jesus who will intercede. Each skit should project how Jesus would treat these people, what he would say to them, and how the excluded person/people would respond to Jesus. Also include what Jesus would say to the people who think they are on the inside. Share the skits.

5. **RESPOND** 6-8 minutes

Draw attention back to the Connect activity with the M&M's. Ask: *What would Jesus say to those who had few M&M's? What would Jesus say to those who had a lot of M&M's?* (Remember, the people who would have gotten the most M&M's were those who said they felt like outsiders, and people lost M&M's if they had *treated* others as outsiders.) Find out who was the person with the most M&M's. Give them the leftovers and a big hug!

Wrap up by saying: *Remember we are God's children, creatures of the Creator. It's not the world who determines whether or not you are an insider, but it is the faith and love we share that brings us "inside" the community of God.*

Close in prayer, asking God to help each one see and accept themselves and others as insiders in God's community of grace.

INSIGHTS FROM SCRIPTURE

>>>
LOOK AHEAD

For Session 5, ask one of the participants to become familiar with the story of Shadrach, Meshach, and Abednego (Daniel 3:10-30) so they can retell it in their own words.

Human beings want and need connection and belonging. If that doesn't happen, people attempt to meet those needs in unhealthy ways. In gangs, for example, a person will do anything to support the gang, even stabbing or shooting someone. Boys & Girls Clubs of America, for one, offer youth an opportunity to belong and experience care and acceptance in a safe and healthy environment.

The faith community also offers a place to belong, to be accepted and cared for. To be "in," one only needs to be willing to love, admit mistakes (that you're not perfect), and accept God's grace. Is your faith community filled with people who don't "sort" or put people into "classes"? Does it help and welcome others into the community of grace God has created for us? The Bible stories from Luke 7 and Matthew 9 shed more light on the qualities of this community.

>> HEALING STIGMA AND SHAME

Simon, the Pharisee, invites Jesus to his home, knowing his reputation as a prophet. A woman comes in and begins to cry on Jesus' feet, wiping them with her hair. Simon, judging a disreputable woman, is surprised that Jesus let her touch him (Luke 7:36-50). With cultural, social (notorious reputation), psychological, and spiritual strikes against her, she has given up trying to fit into a community that had already written her off. What has she left to lose by breaching this barrier? Finally, she ignores the rigid boundaries by stepping in to wash Jesus' feet, an act praised by Jesus even as the host complains.

This woman showed Jesus her love *because* she was forgiven, not *in order* to be forgiven. Because she had been so well forgiven, she was overcome with gratitude, and was thus brought into the new community of grace, a place where many who were on the outside were brought inside. They were restored to God and accepted into God's fellowship. Others who *thought* they were on the inside, thinking of themselves as already righteous, were incensed to find others invited into the fold. Admitting that we all need forgiveness puts us on a more equal footing, more ready to forgive each other, and thus change lives.

>> MATTHEW

He was most likely a toll gatherer near Capernaum on a caravan route just north of the Sea of Galilee. He would sit beside the road and tax export products such as fish and salt. As a toll gatherer, Matthew was despised by Jews for extracting taxes for the occupation government, and because his trade usually involved corruption and extortion. His "dirty" money was not accepted in the offering plate, and therefore he could not be considered righteous. His testimony in a court of law was also unacceptable; his word was no good. Matthew was a Jew, but he was also an outcast.

Jesus probably knew Matthew and had somewhat of a friendship with him. Jesus' plain-spoken call, "follow me," compelled Matthew to follow. Matthew's desire to be "inside" and belong gave him strength to overcome his "professional" life and follow.

Jesus then went and shared food with Matthew and other sinners. Why would Jesus do such a thing? He was/is here for *those who are in need*. Jesus treated "outsiders"—needy, cast-off people—with love and respect, resulting in changed lives. It is the faith and love a person shares that saves them and brings them "inside" the community of God. It's not who you know, what you know, or who you are. It is what you do with "whose you are"! Today, even when we feel outside of God's love and cast off by peers, we, too, can be restored to God. When we respond to God's love, God's love wells up in us all the more.

>>> **SESSION 5**

CONTENTS UNDER PRESSURE >>>

>> KEY VERSES

Nebuchadnezzar said, "Blessed be the God of Shadrach, Meshach, and Abednego, who has sent his angel and delivered his servants who trusted in him. They disobeyed the king's command and yielded up their bodies rather than serve and worship any god except their own God." (Daniel 3:28)

>> FAITH STORY

Daniel 3:10-30; 6:7-28

>> FAITH FOCUS

Daniel, Shadrach, Meshach, and Abednego underwent the ultimate in peer pressure; they faced death because they would not betray their God and follow King Nebuchadnezzar's religious laws. Each time God kept them safe because of their faithfulness. Pressure comes on us from many directions, yet Daniel and his friends were able to resist the pressure and remain true to their values and their God.

>> SESSION GOAL

With many tugs at their loyalties, participants need help to see faithfulness to God as their strength and shield against the onslaught of pressure.

TEACHING PLAN

1. FOCUS 5-6 minutes

>> **Option A:** Put the donuts out on a table. Tell everyone they have one chance at getting a donut. Have everyone divide themselves into three groups (don't assign groups if you can help it) with at least one person in each group. Assign three different areas for each group, numbering them 1, 2, and 3. If a group ends up with only one person, that's okay. First, everyone in group #1 must do 20 jumping jacks. If everyone does not participate, no one in that group will get a donut. If everyone participates, **then each person may take a donut and eat it**, but don't tell them this until after they do the jumping jacks. For group #2, each person must recite a poem or sing a song. Once they do they can have a donut. If someone chooses not to participate, they are the **only** one refused a donut. People in group #3 may each help themselves to one donut apiece, no requirements.

>> Materials needed and advance preparation

- Donuts, enough for one per participant (*Option A* in Focus)

- Candle, fire, or warm room for Explore the Bible section

- Recruit one participant to tell the Daniel 3:10-30 story in their own words (*Option B* in Explore)

- Bibles

- Pieces/shapes of paper of eight different colors, enough for each person to choose two of their favorite colors (*Option B* in Apply)

- Newsprint/markers or chalkboard/chalk

- Copies of the handout sheet for Session 5, folded in half lengthwise

- Writing paper/pencils

In Real Life | A Speck in the Universe   29

Go on to Connect *Option A*, below.

>> **Option B:** Have everyone reflect for a minute on the many different decisions, large and small, they made over the last week. For example, participants who drive make decisions each second with regard to starting, stopping, switching lanes, etc. Give everyone a sheet of paper and pencil. Tell them they have three minutes to write down as many of those decisions as they can think of. Start them, then stop them at the end of three minutes. Chances are they could have kept writing for hours.

Go on to Connect *Option B*, below.

> "Thus once again the story embraces unlikelihood; the impossible comes to pass. The lesson? No one lies outside the swath of providence; even a criminal ruler may be saved. The God of the faithful ones has worked yet another wonder; the oppressor too is 'delivered.'"
>
> Daniel Berrigan, S.J.
> *Daniel: Under the Seige of the Divine*

2. CONNECT 4-6 minutes

>> **Option A:** Ask the following questions:

- *Did everyone participate? Why or why not?*
- *If you did participate, what were your motivations?*
- *If you didn't participate, why didn't you?*
- *Did you like the group you chose (you did choose your group, remember)? Why or why not?*
- *What would you do differently if you were to do this activity again?*
- *Were you always in control of whether or not you got a donut?*

>> **Option B:** Now mark the decisions (some may get more than one mark):

- **Star** the most important decision you made in the last few days.
- **Underline** decisions you made because someone else wanted you to decide that way.
- **Circle** decisions you made that were contrary to what your peers wanted.
- **Squiggle** under decisions that you think will make you feel good about yourself in the future.
- **Cross out** decisions that you think might erode your self-confidence and/or, looking back, were poor decisions.

Shift to the next activity by saying: *Every day we have to make decisions, some easy, some hard. Pressure seems to come from all sides—parents, peers, teachers, coaches, church; everyone wants a piece of you. Can your faith relieve some of the pressure?*

3. EXPLORE THE BIBLE 15-20 minutes

In getting ready to read and act out the story of Shadrach, Meshach, and Abednego, prepare with one of the following:

1. Light a candle, place it where all can see.
2. Locate yourselves around a fire, either outdoors or by a fireplace.
3. Heat up a room in your church or go to the boiler room (if such a place exists).

Ask people if they have ever gotten burned, or how much heat the human body can tolerate before it starts to break down. Then announce that there will be a quiz after the Bible work, so pay attention!

>> **Option A:** Read and act out the account of Shadrach, Meshach, and Abednego in Daniel 3:10-30. The group members are the actors, while you read. As you go, if there is action, have the "actors" do the action. If there is a speaking part, have them repeat it

after you read it. If they need more oomph, encourage them with something like: *Give it more feeling, the king was FURIOUS!* Repeat things if necessary until they are getting into their parts. This can help participants get past their inhibitions. As you go and need more people, incorporate more participants. You don't need to give them an option, just grab them and say, *We need more guards, you'll do just fine!*

Go on to *For Both Options*, below.

》 **Option B:** Arrange to have someone in the group *tell* (in their own words) the Shadrach, Meshach, and Abednego story (Daniel 3:10-30) to the group *without* using the Bible. Let them use notes or rewrite it if they want to. Ask them to include details and be as accurate as possible.

Go on to *For Both Options*, below.

》 **For Both Options:** Next ask everyone to read in their Bibles Daniel 6:7-28, the story of Daniel in the lion's den. Again inform them to pay attention to details because there will be a quiz later. When everyone is finished, ask them what they learned about Daniel. List these things on the chalkboard/newsprint. Ask:

- *What choices or options did Shadrach, Meshach, Abednego, and Daniel have?*
- *What were the consequences?*
- *What saved them?*

Distribute copies of the handout sheet with the Obvious Quiz and give everyone time to take it.

4. APPLY 10 minutes

》 **Option A:** Now have the participants take the Real Life Quiz on the other half of the handout. After everyone is finished, ask:

- *How do you feel about yourself when you trust God to take care of you?*
- *Do you always do what you feel God wants you to do? Why or why not?*
- *If your peers are pressuring you to do one thing and you know God wants you to do another, what do you do? Why would someone choose to follow their peers?*
- *What would help you be more faithful to God, help you rely on and trust God more fully?*

Have a couple of people share their responses to questions 6 and 7 from the quiz.

Read Matthew 6:24. Ask:

- *What does it mean that you cannot "serve two masters"?*
- *What happens when you try to please everyone?*

》 **Option B:** Call attention to the piles of colored shapes you prepared, and invite each participant to choose their favorite **two** colors and then sit back down with their paper shapes. Tell them to imagine that from now on they'll only buy clothes, accessories, etc., that are predominantly the two colors they chose. Discuss: *How would that affect how you shop? where you shop? how often? how long it takes?* Some people in the group may be aware of the technique of "color analysis"; once people decide which color best fits with their skin tone, they shop for just that color palette and can ignore clothing that isn't the "right" color for them. If it doesn't come out in discussion, point out that once they've made some of the big decisions, it narrows down the choices for later decisions. Shadrach, Meshach, Abednego, and Daniel chose God, so it made other decisions clearer.

5. RESPOND 10 minutes

>> **Option A:** Give participants a way to analyze their important decisions by making the following chart. Distribute paper and pencils, and have them think of a decision they will need to make or a situation they will be confronted with in the near future. This "trial dilemma" will be the heading of their paper. Then have them make five columns.

- In Column 1: *List (and number) options for dealing with the dilemma.*
- In Column 2: *What consequences or outcomes may occur with each option?*
- In Column 3: *Who is being served in each option?*
- In Column 4: *How will you feel about yourself in regard to the various options?*
- In Column 5: *Where is support from others in each option?*

Say: *Now choose your option by putting a star beside it. Why did you choose it?*

Close by reminding everyone of the faith and trust Shadrach, Meshach, and Abednego had in God, the desire Daniel had to be faithful to God, and how God cared for them. Reassure them that God is with them, that God will respond when they are faithful. Let them know there are people in the church family who care about them, and with whom they can talk when they feel crushed by the pressure from others. Close with prayer, asking God to be visible and present as we wrestle with pressures and decisions in life.

>>> MORE RESOURCES

Other resources for decision making with youth:

- *Mindtools.com* includes strategies and considers the impact of values and ethics.

- *Option Plays* by Chap Clark, Duffy Robbins, and Mike Yaconelli includes hypothetical dilemmas to help youth practice effective decision making.

- *Tension Getters I* or *II* has a number of real-life problems with which youth can wrestle.

INSIGHTS FROM SCRIPTURE

Shadrach, Meshach, and Abednego were three young companions of Daniel's, all Jews. Because they were young—probably not much older than your youth—strong, skillful, smart, and without blemish, they were groomed to serve in the palace of the Babylonian king, Nebuchadnezzar. Their story is one of unfaltering faith and devotion to the God of Israel. The pressure they faced must have been all the stronger because they had been treated so well. Even the names by which we know them were not their Israelite names, but were names given them by the palace master.

But when the trumpets sounded, they would not worship an idol. Picture hundreds of people, among them leaders of the kingdom, kneeling over, faces in the dust while these three stand like three trees in a field of rocks. They were well aware of the king's decree, the pressure put on people to worship the image. They also refused to worship any person or object. Instead, they placed their trust in the Lord with *no* assurances of how God would respond. They were committed, however, to the covenant with God, and the commandments. They knew they could not second-guess God. All they had was healthy self-esteem and faith and trust to put themselves into God's hands.

So these well-bred, well-educated young men were sentenced to the furnace. We need not take literally the note that the fire was heated "seven times hotter" to get the idea that the fire was indeed so hot that several of the king's soldiers died from the heat putting Shadrach, Meshach, and Abednego into the flames. When King Nebuchadnezzar saw they were still alive, he was so astonished that he condemned instead any blasphemy against the God of Shadrach, Meshach, and Abednego. Because of their witness, we have a picture of a king who very nearly converted to the God of the Jews. The completion of that job was left to Daniel and to God (chapter 4).

>> DANIEL HOLDS FAST

Daniel, who had distinguished himself in the courts of both Nebuchadnezzar and his son Belshazzar, was given prominent position in the court of another king, Darius. Out of jealousy, Daniel's contemporaries at court tried to find fault with him, so as to ruin his favor with the king. Daniel's "fault" was that he would not be pressured into praying to the king, something that went against his faith. Though the king was distraught at being tricked into condemning Daniel, he could not do anything to save Daniel without losing face. So Daniel was put into the lion's den. The next day the king rejoiced that Daniel was still alive and put to death those who had reported Daniel in the first place.

In both stories the faithful followers of God were kept safe. They would not yield to the pressure of worshiping or praying to another god, even if it meant losing their lives. They were strong in their faith, for they knew the consequences were far worse if they went against the Way of God. They also knew God's love and care would never end. Daniel and his friends were able to resist the pressure.

>> GENERATION WHY UNDER PRESSURE

Youth have a strong need to belong and be part of a group, so many of their decisions are based on meeting this need. Yet they also long to distinguish themselves. When youth are faced with the question *Are you a Christian or not?* will they be able to stand up for it under pressure? With healthy self-esteem and the support of a Christian community, they can. We all need people to encourage our faith and reinforce decisions based on faith and trust in God.

Your task is to help participants identify the pressures that come with making decisions, the options they have, the consequences that could follow, and to remind them that relying on God does not mean they will always get what they want. They will undoubtedly ask the next logical question: *What's in it for me, then?* Sometimes it feels that God requires a lot of us, but it is hard to see the divine rewards. Some rewards we will see and understand, others we won't.

Two things we *will* receive: peace of mind knowing we are being faithful to God, and a sense of belonging to a God who is more powerful and loving than anything we know. In that, we receive self-esteem, knowing we did the right thing. God will be faithful, even if the outcome isn't what we had in mind.

>> LOOK AHEAD

For one of the options in next session's Focus, you'll need to locate a tree stump or log, or large bucket (in other words, something to stand on for "Ruler of the Hill"). Also bring a deck of cards, and a candy bar to give away.

Another OBVIOUS Quiz

Circle the answer(s) which is (are) closest to the truth.

1. Shadrach, Meshach and Abednego were:
   a. the real first names of Beatles (two of them shared a name).
   b. popular names for used car salespeople in Brazil.
   c. also known as Myshack, Yourshack, and Bungalow.
   d. Jewish people of long ago who refused to worship an idol of gold.

2. Nebuchadnezzar:
   a. hated to spell or write his name.
   b. was never in the papers because his name was always misspelled.
   c. was so angry with Meshach, Shadrach, and Abednego that he had the fire heated up seven times its normal temperature.
   d. was really a nice guy if you got to know him.

3. The fire was so hot it:
   a. cooked enough hotdogs for an entire city.
   b. roasted a turkey faster than a microwave oven.
   c. kept setting the marshmallows on fire.
   d. killed an undisclosed number of soldiers who threw the Jews in.

4. Shadrach, Meshach, and Abednego were saved from the fire because:
   a. they trusted their God.
   b. they wore their special flame-retardant pajamas.
   c. they trusted their God.
   d. they drank a lot of fluids to keep from getting dehydrated.
   e. they trusted their God.
   f. they lived in the desert and were used to the dry heat.
   g. they trusted their God.

5. Daniel made King Darius mad because:
   a. he continually mispronounced his name.
   b. he would hang on the rim after slam-dunking the basketball on the king's court.
   c. he would only pray to God, not to King Darius.
   d. he kept sticking his bubblegum on the bottom of the king's chair.

6. Daniel was not eaten by the lions because:
   a. the lions had a big supper of carbohydrates the night before.
   b. the lions did not like red meat; it elevated their cholesterol levels.
   c. Daniel shut his eyes, pretended to hide, and it worked!
   d. God sent an angel who protected Daniel.

7. King Darius:
   a. was so glad Daniel lived he decreed that everyone was to worship Daniel's God.
   b. got upset, fired the lion's coach, moved them to Detroit, and invented cheerleaders.
   c. made sure they put barbecue sauce on the next person to go into the den.
   d. traded the lions for a few good piranhas.

Exploring tough questions facing youth today

The Real Life Quiz

Circle all that apply to/in your life.

1. I involve God in my decisions:
   a. all the time
   b. some of the time.
   c. once in a while.
   d. when I'm in real need.
   e. never.

2. I trust God:
   a. all the time.
   b. when it suits me.
   c. on decisions that I have no control over.
   d. never to help me.
   e. always to help me.
   f. Other _____

3. The decisions I've made in my life have:
   a. really not affected my life one bit.
   b. changed everything about my life.
   c. been made by myself.
   d. been made after I see what my friends would do.
   e. been made after talking with adults.

4. I find the story of Shadrach, Meshach, and Abednego:
   a. encouraging because God saved them.
   b. amazing because of their faith.
   c. encouraging because they had intestinal fortitude and stuck with their beliefs.
   d. has no redeemable value.
   e. depressing; I can never have that much faith.

5. I make decisions based on my faith and belief in God:
   a. 10 or more times a day.
   b. 5-9 times a day.
   c. 1-4 times a day.
   d. 5 times a week.
   e. Less than once a week.

6. List reasons why people don't always trust God when they make decisions and choices:
   _____
   _____
   _____

7. List one situation where you trusted God in a decision and how God responded:
   _____
   _____
   _____

A Speck in the Universe : Session 5

Permission is granted to photocopy this handout for use with this session.

》》 **SESSION 6**

HUMILITY AND SELF-CONFIDENCE 》》

》》 KEY VERSE

He has brought down the powerful from their thrones, and lifted up the lowly. (Luke 1:52)

》》 FAITH STORY

Luke 1:26-56

》》 FAITH FOCUS

Mary, a young girl, was visited by an angel who told her she would get pregnant with the son of God. Though perplexed, Mary accepted the task of being the Messiah's mother, submitting herself to God's plan. Mary's story is about strong self-esteem as well as about humility. Her trust in God and her healthy self-esteem allowed her to be strong through the whole ordeal of being the mother of a misunderstood Christ.

》》 SESSION GOAL

For true strength, help participants develop humility and self-confidence based on being committed children of God.

》》 Materials needed and advance preparation

- Tree stump, large bucket, or log, and a candy bar (*Option A* in Focus)
- Chalkboard/chalk or newsprint/markers
- Deck of cards (*Option C* in Focus)
- Bibles
- Copies of handout sheet for Session 6

 **TEACHING PLAN**

1. FOCUS 12-14 minutes

Choose **two** of the following options:

》 **Option A:** Play "Ruler of the Hill." Using a tree stump, bucket, or log, ask if there is one person who thinks they can stay on top without being knocked off. If they can stay on, they get a candy bar. Give everyone a chance to stay on, others a chance to knock them off. After everyone who wishes has tried, ask:

- *What kind of person does it take to stay on top?*
- *What kind of person does it take to knock someone off?*
- *What motivated you to try?*
- *If you didn't try to stay on or knock someone off, why?*

In Real Life | A Speck in the Universe   35

>> **Option B:** Have participants brainstorm a list of people they view as being successful (try to include actors/actresses, business people, political figures, athletes, church leaders, etc.). Write their names on newsprint or a chalkboard. Ask the following questions:

- *What made these people successful?*
- *How did they get to where they are today?*
- *Which of their personality traits or characteristics helped them get where they are today?*
- *Is there any difference between these people and yourself? If so, what?*
- *What does a successful person have that others don't?*

>> **Option C:** Play a couple of rounds of "Hearts" (put people into groups of two or three to keep things moving, so there would be about six hands in the game) with one variation. The person with the two of clubs can make up a new rule which is in effect for that round. This rule can pertain to the card game, or it can be directed toward a person or group of people to make their lives temporarily miserable (for example—all those who have diamonds in their hands must do 20 jumping jacks, the oldest person with blue eyes gets their score doubled, etc.). When you are finished, ask:

- *How did it feel to be in control of others?*
- *How did it feel to be controlled by someone else?*
- *Which person who had the two of clubs would you want as a dictator? Why?*
- *Who wouldn't you want as a dictator? Why?*

"i can remember my father arguing for a lowercase jesus years ago. he felt that self-centeredness was the original sin and that the humility jesus exemplified was a core criterion for the christian life."

David Waas

2. CONNECT 10 minutes

In our society, there are many different messages about what a person needs and how they should behave to be somebody and get somewhere. Have your group list on the board/newsprint the messages they hear that tell them what it takes to get on top, what society says it takes to "really be somebody." When things start to slow down, summarize by saying: *So North American culture would say to be on top, to really be somebody, you must be...* (fill in with the things listed). Were the words "humility" or "humble" included in the list? If not, write in big letters the word "humility" somewhere in the midst of all the other things. Ask:

- *Does anyone know what "humility" means?*
- *Name a humble person you know or have heard of.*
- *Would being humble help you make it to the top in North American culture? Why or why not?*

Shift to the next activity by saying: *In a culture where humility is rare, it can be hard for us to incorporate it into our own lives, especially if we are trying to get ahead. Let's look at what the Bible has to say to us about humility.*

3. EXPLORE THE BIBLE 15-18 minutes

Explain that you are going to read a story and you would like everyone to shut their eyes and listen. While you read you will ask them to put themselves in the place of the young girl, trying to feel what she felt, to respond the way she might respond. Read Luke 1:26-56, in which Mary is visited by the angel and her response and sharing with Elizabeth. When finished, keeping their eyes shut, ask participants the following questions:

- *How do you think Mary felt about the angel's visit?*
- *What options did she have?*
- *How did she respond to the angel? Elizabeth? God?*
- *What was Mary's attitude toward herself? God?*
- *Where did Mary get her strength?*

Invite everyone to open eyes. Write the following Bible passages on newsprint or the chalkboard, divide into four groups, and have each group take a different passage (or look at the passages together if you have just a few people). From the passages, each group is to come up with a definition for *humility*.

- 1 Peter 5:1-10
- Philippians 2:1-11
- Romans 12:3-10
- Colossians 3:12-15

Ask the following questions:

- *What guidance do these passages offer in regard to humility?*
- *What should our attitude be like (Phil. 2:5)?*
- *What does Colossians 3:12 say about our dress?*
- *How are we to consider ourselves (Phil. 2:3)?*
- *What does Romans 12:2 say about the world and how we relate to it?*
- *What do we receive for being humble (1 Peter 5:5)?*
- *Why do you think humility is so important in life?*

List the responses on newsprint or the chalkboard.

"There is something in humility which strangely exalts the heart."

St. Augustine

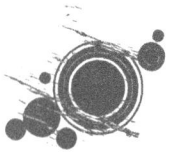

4. APPLY 6-8 minutes

Read the following **twice**. Ask participants to listen to the possible responses the first time, then to raise their hands the second time on the one they relate to the most.

As a child of God, where is humility in your life? What is your attitude toward humility? Do you experience it like:

- *air—breathing it in several times a minute*
- *water—taking five or six good drinks a day*
- *food—partaking three balanced meals a day*
- *sleep—dwelling on it once a day for an extended period of time*
- *shower—once a day is enough, brisk and cleansing with a little shampoo, conditioner, and soap*
- *school—five days a week, with weekends, summers, and holidays off*
- *church—once a week if I have to*
- *visit to the dentist—twice a year for a cleaning, thank you*
- *the plague—never would be just fine*
- *braces—for an extended intense period of time, it's going to hurt, but I need straightening out*

Write these four words on the newsprint or chalkboard—***arrogance, self-confidence, humility, strength***—then ask: *How are these concepts different from each other? How are they related?* If it doesn't come out in discussion, suggest that arrogance is not the same as self-confidence, but healthy self-confidence is required for true strength and humility.

"What does the root hum- mean? It must have to do with humble, or with humilis, humiliate. Those words come from roots meaning 'of the ground, lowly.' But humus does not refer to the ground itself. It refers to the end product of decaying litter and dead creatures. It also has to do with being humorous, that is, in the original meaning, 'wet.' Both people and humus are wet inside. Wetness is opportunity. It represents the openness of nature to what falls from heaven. As Meister Eckhart put it, the humble [one] is '[the one] who is watered with grace.'"

William Bryant Logan, *Dirt: The Ecstatic Skin of the Earth*

5. RESPOND 5 minutes

To close, distribute copies of the handout sheet, "Affirmation of Humility." Assign the various parts to individuals (or groups) and give everyone a minute to read it to themselves. Then as a group, read the affirmation and commitment form. When finished, have everyone sign and get two "witness" signatures. Encourage them to keep it visible, someplace at home or school.

# INSIGHTS FROM SCRIPTURE

When Mary was a girl, barely a young woman, she was visited by an angel who told her she would be the mother of God's son. In Luke's gospel, all of history hinges on the choice of a single teenage girl who is willing to risk disdain and even death to say "yes" to God. With a humble and trusting attitude, she would bear a child named Jesus. Her response was to say yes to God's will and rejoice. She knew being chosen would be her strength.

Does Mary feel she has a free choice to join this drama? She describes herself as a slave (*doulē*), yet she has a say in the matter. God does not force her to say yes. She could have said no, but she didn't. Mary takes on the role so thoroughly that she embodies what she sings—asserting that God raises the lowly highlights the difference between being *God's* slave and being a slave in the Roman world. It's a powerful metaphor and paradox. In the new covenant, to be a "slave" of God is to find a power completely antithetical to the reality of slavery in the Roman empire.

Inner strength, strong self-esteem, knowing who and whose you are, gives one the ability to face peer pressure. Contrary to a "wimpish" image, true humility, undergirded by strong self-esteem, is empowering. At the same time, it does not overwhelm others, it is not arrogant, boastful, or rude. Mary's story is a good wrap-up for a unit on self-esteem because it highlights the benefits of healthy self-esteem: humility, strong servanthood, courage in the face of pressure, a confident voice of truth. Mary was humble not so much because she lay down and took whatever God handed her, but because her trust in God and her self-esteem allowed her to be strong through the blessing and ordeal of being the mother of a misunderstood Christ.

HUMILITY UNDERGIRDED BY TRUE STRENGTH

Humility was also a favorite theme in letters to early Christian churches. Often these fledgling groups faced power struggles as leaders did their best to guide new believers. Humility was essential for the church to survive. Without it there was division, and divided, the church would lose strength and ultimately collapse.

Paul, in his greeting to the Roman churches, called himself a "servant," which in the Greek is *doulos* or "slave." In Jesus' time there were many who were slaves in homes of the rich, but they had status and responsibility, much like modern-day servants. Their attitude was that of a servant, working to help maintain the household. It was done with devotion to the master. Servants were humble, not exercising power over others, not being served, but taking the initiative to serve. Their strength and power was rooted in being a servant.

›› HUMILITY IS COUNTERCULTURE

In North American culture, humility and an attitude of service are rare traits. Economies are driven by consumption, so businesses have to capitalize on self-centeredness, and often bolster the individual with no concern for the community. Youth hear these messages. They are especially vulnerable because they are at a stage in life when it is natural to be self-centered. Humility is one of the last things on their mind. They want to be in control, they want power (horsepower even). They are beginning to have control and power over their own lives as they practice increasing independence.

Another message often sent by the media is that arrogance equals high self-esteem. Swaggering movie characters may look appealing to someone with an unhealthy self-esteem. They appear to have control and power over others. Unlike the connection of humility with a healthy self-esteem, arrogance is at best a flaunting of self-centeredness. At worst it is dangerous disregard for others.

Youth might sneer at the idea of being humble, or wonder how it is possible to be humble without feeling humiliated. Being humble in North American society goes against the cultural grain, and it can be hard for youth to see a bright future in it. Yet Mary says it all in her example as Christ's mother. She willingly accepted her call from God and so received strength. Young people today can also receive strength through living in a humble way.

With God, *giving up* power and control is *getting* power and control. When you don't have anything, you can have everything. When you don't have anything, who can pressure you? When you are God's humble and willing servant, who can control you? Jesus is our model for humility and self-confidence, giving up everything, even his life, to gain life for all (Phil. 2:1-11).

Affirmation of Humility

ALL:	We humanoid, carbon-based life forms,
Reader 1:	participants in this faith community,
Reader 2:	residents of the North American continent,
Reader 3:	located on the third planet from a star in the Milky Way galaxy
ALL:	which is part of the universe created by a wonderful, powerful, awesome, one-and-only God,
Reader 2:	in whose image, by the way, we are created, and with whose glory we are crowned,
ALL:	do hereby affirm
Reader 1:	(we don't swear)
ALL:	to faithfully practice being a humble people,
Reader 3:	being strengthened in our humility to lift up the gifts in others,
Guys:	responding out of respect and not conceit,
Girls:	promising not to act like the center of the universe any longer,
ALL:	not to be loud,
Adult leader:	practicing quieting ourselves at least once a day with our Creator,
Reader 2:	striving to care for others,
Reader 3:	becoming increasingly conscious
Reader 1:	(as opposed to unconscious)
ALL:	of how our actions affect others in our homes, schools,
Reader 1:	churches, communities,
Reader 2:	states/provinces, continent,
Reader 3:	world, solar system,
Adult leader:	galaxy, and universe.
ALL:	May we always be humble in the presence of our God
Readers 1, 2, 3:	(who, by the way, is everywhere and all the time!).
ALL:	Amen and Amen!

Signed_____ Date_____

Witnessed by _____ & _____

A Speck in the Universe :: Session 6

Permission is granted to photocopy this handout for use with this session.

>>> EXTENDER SESSION
(best used after Session 1)

COMMUNITY STARGAZING

>> SESSION GOAL

Since youth often struggle with identity and a sense of self-worth, help them see how, though we are mere specks in the universe, we are created "very good," worthy to be here, and are intimately connected to the Creator who made such an amazing universe.

>> PLAN

On a clear, moonless night, take the group to a place away from city lights, lie out under the stars on sleeping bags, plastic bags, or tarps and listen to *The Planets* by Gustav Holst while gazing up into the night sky. If possible, invite someone from the parish who is familiar with constellations and can point some out to everyone. While people lie there, have them ponder:

- how far the light has traveled from each star
- how big the universe is
- the greatness of God who created the universe
- being created in God's image
- what it would be like to travel in space
- what their role is in the scheme of things
- (add some of your own)

Read Psalm 8 as you stargaze, and point out how, though we are mere specks in the universe, we are created "very good," worthy to be here, and are intimately connected to the Creator who made such an amazing universe.

In Real Life
Exploring tough questions facing youth today

CLUELESS AND CALLED
Discipleship and the Gospel of Mark

What does it take to be a disciple? This study of the Gospel of Mark focuses on the requirements for following Jesus' way and the abundant life that is ours as a result. (5 sessions)

DO MIRACLES HAPPEN?
Signs and Wonders in the Gospel of John

The greatest miracle, recorded in John 1:14 and 3:16, is the miracle of God's love that became flesh and lived among us. But John also included examples of what we more traditionally think of as miracles: the wonder of abundance from little; healing; signs of impossibility and faith; and the resurrection. (5 sessions)

DO THE RIGHT THING
Ethics Shaped by Faith

How do you know what's right and what's wrong? Even when you figure it out, the right thing is often the unpopular or unpleasant choice. This unit offers participants a clearer sense of what it means to claim a faith identity, a foundation that can help them sort out the gritty details of ethics shaped by faith. (6 sessions)

FIGHT RIGHT
A Christian Approach to Conflict Resolution

This unit will help youth understand conflict and its function. They will learn how they can be honest and loving, and explore how conflict can be used for positive results. They will also learn ways to enhance their communication skills. 1 Corinthians. (5 sessions)

GOD IS A WARRIOR?
Violence in the Bible

The Bible challenges us to be reconciled to one another and work for justice. So what do we do with the stories that seem to condone violence or even encourage it? A discussion of issues in the Old and New Testaments. (6 sessions)

HOW DO YOU KNOW?
Wisdom in the Bible

Wisdom literature teaches us that we gain knowledge of the world, ourselves, and God through experience and observation. This unit provides practical, hands-on wisdom to help young people avoid life's snares and grow closer to God. Proverbs, Job, Ecclesiastes. (5 sessions)

HOW TO BE A TRUE FRIEND
The Bible Reveals Friendship's Heart

To be a friend takes skill. Help youth discover the secrets of friendship through various stories from the Old and New Testament. (6 sessions)

HOW TO READ THE BIBLE
Building Skills for Bible Study

What kind of book is the Bible? What does this book mean to me? This unit looks at the Bible as revelation, as history, as literature. Selected scripture. (5 sessions)

KEEPING THE GARDEN
A Faith Response to God's Creation

If Christians believe that God made the world, we do not need any more compelling reason to care for it than that God has handed us a treasure to hold and protect. This unit gets beyond trendy environmentalism and challenges youth to see environmental awareness as a religious issue. Genesis. (6 sessions)

MANTRAS, MENORAHS, AND MINARETS
Encountering Other Faiths

How is Christianity different from other faiths? Why do others believe the way they do? This study can give youth a new appreciation for the uniqueness of Jesus. Selected scripture. (5 sessions)

SALT, LIGHT, AND THE GOOD LIFE
The Beatitudes and the Sermon on the Mount

What can youth expect in a life of discipleship? This unit explores the Sermon on the Mount under four main sections: the Beatitudes, Salt and Light, Jesus and the Law, and Heavenly Teachings. Matthew 5. (6 sessions)

A SPECK IN THE UNIVERSE
The Bible on Self-Esteem and Peer Pressure

Discover God's unconditional love and acceptance of all people. This study will show positive ways to have one's life make a difference, and help youth find ways to resist negative peer pressure and turn it into positive action. (6 sessions)

THE RADICAL REIGN
Parables of Jesus

Jesus used parables to reveal what the kingdom of God is like, and how God relates to us. This study highlights how the parables reveal God's reign as radically different from the world we live in, and what that means for the Christian life. (6 sessions)

TESTING THE WATERS
Basic Tenets of Faith

Discover the biblical roots for the central Christian concepts of covenant, community, and baptism. This short course is a way to test the (baptismal) waters of Christianity before diving in, or review the basics for those who already have. (6 sessions)

WHO IS GOD?
Engaging the Mystery

God is beyond human comprehension, yet desires to be known. These sessions focus on the way we get clues about and glimpses of God from the Bible, God's creation, and church tradition. Selected scripture. (5 sessions)

www.ingramcontent.com/pod-product-compliance
Lightning Source LLC
Chambersburg PA
CBHW080408170426
43193CB00016B/2860